My Testimonies

Sophia Bygrave

Author's Tranquility Press
ATLANTA, GEORGIA

Copyright © 2023 by Sophia Alecia Bygrave

All rights reserved. No part of this publication may be reproduced, distributed, or transmitted in any form or by any means, including photocopying, recording, or other electronic or mechanical methods, without the prior written permission of the publisher, except in the case of brief quotations embodied in critical reviews and certain other noncommercial uses permitted by copyright law. For permission requests, write to the publisher, addressed "Attention: Permissions Coordinator," at the address below.

Sophia Alecia Bygrave/Author's Tranquility Press
3800 Camp Creek Pkwy SW Bldg. 1400-116 #1255
Atlanta, GA 30331, USA
www.authorstranquilitypress.com

Ordering Information:
Quantity sales. Special discounts are available on quantity purchases by corporations, associations, and others. For details, contact the "Special Sales Department" at the address above.

For workshops, speaking engagements or to order additional copies of this book email Sophia at: *sophiadvisor@gmail.com*

My Testimonies/Sophia Alecia Bygrave
Paperback: 978-1-962492-52-2
eBook: 978-1-962492-53-9

Contents

Dedication
Acknowledgement

Chapter 1:
Introduction 1
Chapter 2:
Instant Healing 3
    Healing from Tonsilitis 3
    Healing from Back Pain 4
    Healing from Earache 6
Chapter 3:
Healing from Digestive Distress 8
Chapter 4:
Healing After Car Accident 12
Your Testimony 18
Chapter 5:
Healing from Conjunctivitis 19
Chapter 6:
Supernatural Bus Trip 22
Your Testimony 25
Chapter 7:

To Move to Jamaica 27
Your Testimony 32

Chapter 8:
Financial Provision 33
Your Testimony 36

Chapter 9:
In His Care 37

Chapter 10:
Miraculous Car Repair 40

Chapter 11:
Amazing Deal 43

Chapter 12:
Miraculous Car Sale 47
Author Contact Page 51

Dedication

This book is dedicated for the glory of God in the Earth.

Acknowledgement

I am thankful for the help that I have received, which has enabled me to complete this book. I am thankful for the constant encouragement and support of my friends as they continue to add rich value to my life.

I am also truly grateful for people like you, who have supported my work by purchasing the books that I have written and contracted me for the workshops that I have given.

Finally, my life has truly been enhanced by persons who have been used by God to be a blessing to me in different ways. To God be all the glory and the praise.

Chapter 1: Introduction

I am excited to tell you about how amazing our God is! This book is written to give glory to God and to be an encouragement to others, many of whom have gone or are going through fiery trials and tribulations.

Each of us has something to give God thanks for. Along life's journey, you have endured and experienced some circumstances, which led you to see the hand of God at work in your life. So, today as you read this book, make every effort to count your blessings.

I have left some pages at the end of some chapters for you to write your own testimonies.

Let us go on this journey together as we seek to celebrate God's goodness and be thankful for the fact that God is always with us. When good things happen, do not forget to give glory to God. It is easy to take the credit when good things happen and forget that God is guiding, providing, and caring for you.

My Testimonies

When we go through adversity, let us take comfort in knowing that with God all things are possible. He is able and willing to turn each adversity into a testimony.

Chapter 2:
Instant Healing

Healing from Tonsilitis

From I was about eight years old, I began to have recurrent tonsillitis. This was a condition in which an infection triggered an inflammation of my tonsils. It usually occurred at the same time every year, which was during the first quarter of each year. When I swallowed, I experienced severe pain and discomfort. It was as painful as a knife cutting in my throat. This continued until I was about eleven years old. At this time, my Church, the Brown's Town Baptist Church, in St. Ann Jamaica, West Indies was having its annual crusade.

This is usually the highlight of the Church's annual calendar. Everyone loved crusades, because the pastor usually invited one or two very charismatic preachers to preach on the Sunday morning and throughout the evenings of that week. It was about March in that year, and while I was a child and the nights were usually cold around that time of year, my family and I walked for half an hour to get to the crusade each night. The sermons were powerful, and the Church was on fire, with shouts of, "Hallelujah!", "Praise the Lord!" and "Amen!" Everybody came in eager anticipation to see and experience miracles!

On one night in particular, the minister preached a hellfire sermon which moved a lot of people to go to the altar for salvation. After the sermon was preached, the minster gave an invitation for people who wanted to receive ministry for healing to come forward. I was one of the first persons to get out of my seat. I was experiencing excruciating pain at that time, so I really wanted to be healed. When he prayed for me, I extended my faith, believing that God would heal me. As soon as he prayed, I felt better. I was healed instantly. Even better than that is the fact that I never had tonsillitis again! That was an instant and permanent work of healing.

During that and other such crusades at the Brown's Town Baptist Church during the 1980s to 1990s, I witnessed many different cases of healing. People with un-even length of legs had the shorter leg grow to the length of the taller leg instantaneously. I saw a dumb lady get healing and began to testify and deaf persons were able to hear what the pastor was saying. Like I said, everyone looked forward to those annual crusades and people came from other parishes in Jamaica to attend those services.

Healing from Back Pain

Early in 1997, I was experiencing severe lower back pain, which was the result of several factors. I had back pains on and off before, but this time the pain was excruciating, and it impeded my daily activities. It was severe and sustained. I had to use a cushion when I sat down, and the pain worsened immensely whenever I was travelling on a bus. As the bus rattled and bumped up and down on the rough surface of the roads, I felt sharp pain shooting down my back and I had to lift my body up off the seat and stay up on my hands until we reached the smoother parts of the road. This discouraged me from travelling unnecessarily. I tried several remedies; ointments, massages, among other things, but nothing really worked.

Thankfully, I knew that the Brown's Town Baptist Church had a special monthly healing and ministry service, called, "Glory in the Church Weekend." This ministry was held one Saturday of every month, and it was offered by Reverend Everard Allen, who has been the pastor there for many years. People travelled from all over the island to get ministry for healing at these services. While the journey from where I lived and studied in St. Andrew in Jamaica, was at least a three- and-a-half-hour drive to Brown's Town, I knew that I had to be there on the next Saturday that this service was being held.

I endured intense pain as I travelled, seemingly endless hours, from St. Andrew to attend the service. Thankfully, I survived the journey, although all of the muscles and joints in my lower back were paining me immensely. If you have ever been on a Country Bus Ride on rugged roads, then you could imagine how I felt. The big bus with worn out shocks, and which was in less than standard working condition, jerked endlessly on the bumpy country roads. The minutes seemed like hours as I propped myself up and groaned and prayed during the three and a half hours drive to Brown's

Town. However, my faith was strong, and I was convinced that I would be healed at that service. There was no other way! I had to be healed because I could not bear the pain anymore.

Finally, we arrived. I entered the Church with eager anticipation of a miracle. When I went to the healing service, I worshipped God with a spirit of expectancy. During the prayer and ministry section at the end of the service I was elated when Reverend Allen called out for persons with pain to come forward for ministry. I was excited because I was taught from early in my Christian life that what God reveals, He will heal. So, I quickly made my way forward to the altar for prayer. Once again, I was healed instantly and was able to testify that I had travelled all the way from St. Andrew to receive my healing. Thankfully, God rewarded my faith and determination to be healed. I knew in my heart that God could heal me, and I did whatever was necessary, disregarding the obstacles and pushed towards receiving my healing.

Healing from Earache

While I was living in Barbados, I became a member of New Dimensions Ministries (NDM). This is a dynamic worship-driven and uplifting Church which is led by Apostle Dr Stephen Holford and Apostle Sandra Holford. When you are in a worship service at NDM, you feel as if you are transported into the actual realms of Heaven. I have been healed and delivered several times during the worship, not to mention being spiritually and emotionally recharged.

Another rich aspect of this Church is that it is centered on Five-Fold Ministry. My life has been truly uplifted and empowered by the apostolic, prophetic ministry of New Dimensions Ministries.

One highlight of the Church's calendar is its annual Apostolic Charismatic Convention, held in July of each year. In 2011, I attended the Convention as I usually did. As one of the guest preachers ministered, I was truly strengthened in my inner man. After the sermon, the preacher called for persons who needed ministry for healing. I had been experiencing intense pains in my left ear for several weeks. Thankfully, sometimes, it was relatively bearable, but I was still believing God for healing.

At the end of his sermon, the minister did some call- out ministry, calling out and praying for specific illnesses. A lot of people went forward for ministry. When this was finished, he asked all the other persons in the Church who needed healing, to just stay where we were and extend our faith. So, that was what I did. The atmosphere was rich with intercession, faith, worship and expectation, and several persons were healed on the spot. From my seat, I lifted my hands to God in faith and pressed in to receive my healing. At that point my ear felt different. After a few minutes had passed, I realized that I had been healed. I went forward in the Church to join all the other persons who had gone up to give their testimonies of healing. It was truly a great experience of God's love, supernatural presence, and power.

Chapter 3:
Healing from Digestive Distress

In 2004, I had one of the most awesome experiences with healing and deliverance ministry.

My first son, Mateo was born after a relatively good pregnancy and an un-complicated delivery. By all accounts, he was a normal healthy baby boy who just needed our love and care. Since he was my first child, and because I had never been around a newborn baby before, I did not know what was normal or abnormal during the first few months of his life. Consequently, I made numerous calls and visits to the doctor and read some relevant books.

Mateo was very colicky and plagued with frequent bouts of vomiting which occurred once or twice most days, especially before he went to sleep at nights. He also had other issues and challenges. It was very distressing to watch him wrestle with his digestive discomforts, especially since they were usually accompanied with prolonged screaming sessions, often followed by the expulsion of copious amounts of vomit. Thankfully, the Lord led us to a very empathetic and experienced doctor; Dr Bullen, who is also a believer. He was a great source of help to us during those difficult months.

By the time he was seven months old, Mateo was using several different kinds of medication each day, some to alleviate coughing, something to alleviate the refluxing and gas, and something to ease the heartburn.

Realizing that I was not coping well with the situation, which often left me feeling overwhelmed and irritable, my husband made arrangements for us to go and see a counsellor. This decision was the first significant move in a series of life changing experiences. This was a great move, because the counsellor that assisted us, Mrs. Walcott - was a born again, Holy Spirit filled believer, who was also involved with deliverance ministry. One day, during one of our one-on-one counselling sessions, she invited me to attend a Women's Aglow International Weekend Retreat, to get a break from my extenuating circumstances and to be spiritually recharged. When the day came for me to attend the retreat, it was a bitter-sweet moment. I was thankful for the break and the opportunity to be spiritually recharged, but it was the first time that I would be apart from Mateo, and I was not happy about that. However, I packed my bags and headed off to the retreat.

My Testimonies

We had to share rooms and as we settled in everyone was so pleasant. We introduced ourselves and were fast friends.

During the ministry, my soul was very refreshed by the Word of God that was shared by the visiting speakers. God was faithful to address all of my spiritual and emotional needs with His Word. By the Saturday afternoon, I kneeled before God and asked Him for a breakthrough in my overwhelming situation. I was too distressed to eat, so I decided to fast my lunch meal and I prayed for a change. I asked God why Mateo was being afflicted with a severe stomach ailment, which I considered to be a curse in my extended family.

Many of my relatives and I had significant digestive disorders. I questioned God because we had repeatedly asked God to cancel all generational curses from passing onto our child throughout my pregnancy.

As I prayed, God revealed some things in my life that I needed to release and reject, and He highlighted some practices that I needed to change. I made a commitment to God to change and to follow Him more closely.

Saturday night, I asked two of the leaders if I could have my husband and my cousin Erica, (who was assisting with Mateo's care) bring Mateo for ministry the next day and they agreed. God had heard my cries for help and was working it all together for our good.

Sophia Bygrave

Sunday afternoon, a visiting speaker, Minister Sonia spoke about Naomi's journey back to Israel after having experienced immense trials and tribulations in Moab, with the loss of her dreams and loved ones. I, like Naomi, was going through a dry and hard place in my life. When the alter call was given, Erica and I took Mateo up for ministry. God showed up and broke the generational curse that was afflicting us. Erica and I were instantly healed and delivered from our own digestive distresses. My cousin and I were plagued with stomach ailments for many years, and we were delivered instantaneously. Mateo was fully set free 21 days later, after I completed a Daniel-Fast, which God had led me to do. Today, my son walks in the fullness of health in Christ. God showed up and rescued us from demonic affliction, which no doctor or medication could have cured.

Since then, I have received deliverance from different oppressive spirits on several occasions, and I have come to realize that sometimes, deliverance is instantaneous but at other times it needs to be done several times for us to gain and retain full deliverance.

Chapter 4:
Healing After Car Accident

In September 2007, while I was living in Barbados, I was on my way to work one bright and beautiful Monday morning. It was the beginning of the new school term, and I was eager to beat the traffic and get to work on time. We usually had an early morning meeting every Monday and my manager and I really did not like it when I arrived late for the meeting. Furthermore, the branch of the company with which I was working, had recently moved to a new location, right in the heart of Bridgetown, St. Michael. This created a bigger challenge than usual to get to work, since I now had to deal with more traffic and a longer drive to get to work.

It was a little after seven in the morning. As I drove along, I got to a roundabout at Haggatt Hall. The traffic usually backed up here at peak traffic hours. After finally getting past that location and as I proceeded down Two-Mile Hill, towards Bridgetown, I got an opportunity to overtake a motorbike, which was going very slowly along the road. I accelerated and was about to pull towards the curb, when a large bus swerved suddenly towards me. Since I was driving fast, in an effort to complete the overtake process, I almost run off the road towards the sidewalk. However, I realized that at the speed and angle I would have run off the road, so I corrected my position and tried to straighten up. By this time another large bus was heading towards me. Given the option to run into a bus full of people or run off the road I made a split- second decision to head for the curb. I had not previously noticed that there was a number of large trees along that portion of the road. So, I ended up running right up the trunk of a tree and this caused the car to overturn, and it landed right onto the top.

In that short time my life felt like I was in a dream. As I heard the rumbling sound of the car scraping against the tree trunk, my heart pounded heavily with terror. All that I could SHOUT as slid out of consciousness was, "Oh, God, HELP!" I believed the power of prayer saved my life that day. I had passed out very briefly from the shock, but I was brought back to consciousness by the sudden jolting of the falling car as it hit the pavement upside-down. As I hung upside- down in the car, I quickly realized that I could have died, or be seriously injured with a severe neck injury or even be paralyzed. I had never been so happy to be in a seatbelt in my life!

When I became alert, I also realized that the front of the car was smoking. I might have damaged the radiator or engine during the impact. After watching many movies where cars caught fire and exploded shortly after crashing, I was not about to stay in that car. I quickly unfastened my seatbelt and began to crawl out of the car. When I reached the sidewalk, several passersby had stopped to see the accident.

Thankfully, as God usually does, He allowed someone who I knew well to be passing on her way to work. Heather Herbert quickly stopped and came to my rescue. I immediately tried to rescue my laptop and valuables in the car and so I asked some of the men to assist me and they did. We moved a safe distance from the car and then I suddenly felt weak, I almost fainted. So, Heather held me up and then sat with me on the sidewalk. A gentleman called the ambulance and the police and notified my family about the accident. I then began to pray. As the shock and my adrenaline induced response dissipated, I finally began to say, "Thank You Jesus, thank You Jesus." A lady who came close to us also began to pray with me. The ambulance came in a few minutes.

As it happened, we were only a short distance away from Barbados' Queen Elizabeth Hospital. By this time, I realized that my chest, back and neck were paining me, so I told the paramedics about it when they questioned me. I still felt faint, so they lifted me onto the stretcher and put me into the ambulance. As they put me into the ambulance and I was groaning in pain, one of them said, "She probably broke her neck." Thankfully, I felt God's peace that passes all understanding. While we were on our way to the hospital, I prayed earnestly against any long-term injury or symptoms from the accident. I did this because a young lady that I worked with had an accident five years before and was still having pains in her back. She had also told us about other persons that she knew that had lingering or recurrent pains after an accident. I did not want any of that. So, I prayed fervently for healing and for God to heal me completely.

In a few minutes, I was at the hospital. As I waited in the Emergency room, the protective headgear that the paramedics had used on me, in the event that I had sustained a head or neck injury, caused excruciating pain in my head. I felt like my head was bursting apart. I called for the nurse, "Nurse, nurse, please help me." When she came, she told me that they could not do anything about the pain until the doctor came to see me. The doctors were doing their morning hospital rounds at that time. After what seemed like forever, a doctor came and examined me. He removed my head-gear and authorized several x-rays to be done right away. Thankfully, after all the examinations were done, I had no broken bones or noticeable injuries. As a matter of fact, the only thing that was visible was a very tiny bruise on one finger. Looking back on the extensive damage that was done to the car, I have often thought that it was as if angels had taken me out of the car and then returned me after the car had crashed, when I jerked back to consciousness. The front of the car was crushed, and the left-hand side was very badly damaged, not to mention the top on which it finally landed. I focused on thanking God for my life and tried not to feel very badly about the lost vehicle, which was too old for comprehensive insurance to cover it.

I was discharged from the hospital after about four hours. God is merciful. I had only sustained some soft tissue damage and some joint discomfort. I rested at home for two weeks and took some anti-inflammatory medication and did some self-help physiotherapy and felt that I was well enough to go back to work, but I was still experiencing chest and neck pains. So, after a week at work, I went on more sick leave.

From early after the accident, God had told me that I was not to wear a neck support, so I did not purchase any. I had to sleep with a soft cushion in the groove of my neck, but this was still painful. The chest pains improved with massage and pain medication, but my neck was still very painful, especially when I moved it suddenly or turned it in some directions. I continued to pray against permanent or long-term injury. By the third week after the accident, I began to do research on whiplash. I concluded that I needed some specialist work to recover properly, but I was confident that God would help.

About the Sunday of the fourth week, I was relaxing in the back of our home. We had designated a playing area for Mateo, our son, to kick ball and play with his toys. It was the coolest part of the house, so I went there to relax and enjoy the evening breeze and read my Bible as Mateo played. I had bent my neck over to read, as this was more comfortable. I was not really concentrating on what Mateo was doing. Suddenly, I felt a firm hit in the back of my neck. I sat up suddenly and then immediately got angry with Mateo for being so careless. I moved away from that area and went to put an ice pack on my neck to alleviate the pain. Then, I became angry with God and asked, "Lord, how could I be reading my Bible and you allow Mateo to kick a football right into my injured neck." I was a bit concerned about what this might do to my neck, but I left it at that. By night-time, I realized that my neck was not paining me anymore. Then it dawned on me that God had allowed Mateo to re-set the some-what dislodged neck vertebrae that was causing the pain in my neck. I was made whole. By the next morning I was certain that I was well. I then realized why God had told me not to wear a neck-supporting brace. If had done this, when Mateo kicked the ball, it would not have made direct contact with my neck vertebrae. After, what seemed like an irrational decision to bear the discomfort instead of supporting my neck, my choice to obey God, was rewarded with the complete resetting of my vertebrae. I told my family what happened and called all my friends to share the good news. I later testified about it at Church and other events.

What seemed like an attack from the enemy when Mateo kicked the ball and hit me on my neck was actually an act of God, which had resulted in the restoration of alignment in my neck. I was healed!

Your Testimony

Chapter 5:
Healing from Conjunctivitis

In early October 2013, I had been experiencing a cold for over two weeks. It was one of those colds that resisted the regular remedies. I still had a runny nose, a cough and a little chest congestion. However, it was not excessively debilitating or overwhelming, so I continued to use my own over-the-counter medications and other remedies.

I was introduced to a new Church in Kinston Jamaica, and I wanted to go to the service the next Sunday. I was told that there would be a really special service that day. I had been praying for healing all throughout my illness. However, symptoms still persisted. On the Thursday of that week, I prayed, fasted, and took authority against every infectious agent and spirit of infirmity and declared that I was healed in Jesus' name. I experienced some relief, but I still had symptoms. However, I believed that it was only a matter of time for the symptoms to clear up. Later that evening, my older son had caught the cold. On the Saturday morning, I prayed with him and commanded the viruses and infectious agents to die and took authority against the spirit of infirmity, in Jesus' name. As soon as I prayed and anointed him, he ran to the bathroom, coughed up some mucus and later returned and said, "I'm feeling better now." Believe it or not, that was the end of his infection and infirmity. Of course, this further stimulated me to intensify my spiritual warfare and declare that I was healed from Thursday and so all symptoms should cease in Jesus' name. However, this did not happen immediately. Never-the-less, I still intended to attend the special Church service the next day.

In the middle of the night, I got up to use the bathroom. As I tried to open my eyes, I realized that my eyelids were sticking together. I panicked a bit, as I remembered the symptoms of Conjunctivitis (Pink Eyes in Jamaica and Red Eyes in Barbados). When I looked into the mirror, my eyes were red, filled with mucus and they were oozing. I bent forward, looked into the mirror and said adamantly, "I do not have Pink Eyes and I was healed already from Thursday." I then cleaned my eyes and went back to sleep. About 4am on Sunday morning, I awoke once more, and again, my eyes were caked together with soggy mucus. When I cleaned them up and looked into the mirror again, they were still red. It was a bit disconcerting; however, I did not give up on my belief that God would heal me. After all, I was looking after children and Conjunctivitis is very infectious. There was just no way that I could have it right now. I was not accepting it that day. I began to intercede and to do some serious spiritual warfare. I then coughed up some much, blew out some through my nostril and anointed myself with consecrated olive oil. I then looked closely into the mirror again and reminded the devil that I was not sick anymore and that I was already healed from that Thursday.

I eventually went back to bed at around five in the morning. When I finally woke up to start the day at close to 7:00 AM, my eyes had cleared up. They were no longer oozing with mucus, and there was only one small red spot in the inner corner of one eye. It was a miracle. I was healed. For the rest of the day, I did not have any cold symptoms and by the following day, my eye had cleared up. God hand honored my resilience in believing Him for healing.

It was like the woman who consistently implored the unjust ruler for justice. Her persistence paid off, and so did mine. As it happened this Church became a very instrumental part of the ministry to which God had called me to do in Jamaica. I soon came to realize that the enemy did not want me to attend that service.

Sometimes, we miss what God has in store for our lives and ministry, because we do not push past the circumstantial appearances, or push past discomforts and difficulties. God wants an army of persons who are strong, people who know who He is, in His power, goodness and faithfulness. We can only experience some of God's supernatural intervention when we choose to wrestle with God and push past peripheral feelings and appearances until we receive our breakthrough! The Word says, "You shall declare a thing and it shall happen." I repeatedly declared that I was healed with no apparent evidence of healing, and I chose to live my faith and not by my sight. When the situation is critical, complaining and worrying will not help. Instead, God is waiting for you to cry out to Him, in faith, not wavering, until He comes through for you.

Chapter 6:
Supernatural Bus Trip

In about 2012, I was working in my own little business, which had just gotten off the ground a few months before. Needless to say, my cash flow was limited. However, I had to do some work on my car. I left it at the garage the day before and they had called to say that it was ready to be collected. I had to take at least two buses to get to the garage.

Unfortunately, where I was living, the buses that would take me in the direction of the garage only passed once per hour. I was just about ready to leave, with just ten minutes to get to the bus stop to catch the bus. As I was putting away some food, the container fell and the entire meal spilled out on the floor, it was too messy to leave until I got back, but I knew immediately, that if I cleaned it up, I would have most likely missed the bus. I was angry. I started to pray and rebuked the devil, because, I needed to get and use the car, and if I had to wait for another hour, the garage would close before I was able to get there. I then rebuked the devil and cleaned up the mess. It was close to 2:00 PM.

Even though I knew that I would not be likely to arrive at the bus stop in time to catch the bus, I still went there. I was worried and concerned. It was a dilemma. When I arrived at the bus stop, somebody from a shop nearby confirmed that the bus had just left. However, I stayed there and prayed and hoped to see someone that I might know, driving by (a very rare occasion). After about ten minutes, an empty bus drove towards me and I waved for it to stop, and it did.

When I stepped in the driver immediately chided me and said, "You missed the bus." I said, " Just barely." However, I had a situation and had to get to the nearest place where I could get a connecting bus to go to the garage. I had told him exactly where I needed to go and that I needed to get there as soon as possible. Thankfully, he decided to take me to the nearby bus terminal, where other buses were leaving for various destinations. That was a blessing because he was technically off route, so he didn't have to pick me up.

When I arrived at the bus terminal, he helped me to find another bus, which would pass exactly where I needed to go. I had not even thought about using that route before, since I did not know all of the bus routes. However, this would be an even shorter route than what I was planning to take. As it happened, a bus was just leaving out, which would pass exactly in front of the garage. It just needed to divert to pick up some passengers on its route and then it would take me there. I was really amazed. Not only did I get a bus that was going where I needed to go, but I got one that would have saved me time and money. It was now clear to me that

God had seen my situation and had turned my adversity into a miraculous experience.

The other part of the story is that I was also praying that the cost for the work that was done on my car would not exceed what I was able to pay. When I arrived at the garage, the staff made the final arrangements to return my car and handed me the bill, unbelievably, it was just the amount that I had put aside to look after the car. I had rolled the money together and placed it in an envelope. It was not a cent more or less. That was supernatural discernment! I really felt like I was in Divine care that day. I truly felt loved and cared for by my Heavenly Father that day. In these seemingly little ways, God showed me that He was interested in the tiniest details of my life. Whatever, it is that is needed, "let your request be made known to God." Expect the impossible. Step out in faith and petition God to work it out for you. I did not have any friends that were available to help me that afternoon, but God is a loving father and a faithful friend, and he came to my rescue. As His children we are in His care as long as we live in obedience, with reverence, faith and in faithfulness.

Your Testimony

Chapter 7:
The Move to Jamaica

Through a combination of dreams and prophetic ministry, God had revealed to me that He wanted me to leave Barbados and return to reside in my homeland, Jamaica. By June of 2013, I felt that it was an opportune time to relocate. This required packing and shipping my possessions and getting things organized to get my sons into school in Jamaica.

It was a big job, but I felt the strength of God each day, as I packed, closed accounts, put important things in place and made the necessary adjustments. I was just barely able to finish packing in time for the shipping company representatives to collect my belongings. In fact, when they came to our home in St. Philip Barbados, I was still running and pushing things into boxes, chest of drawers and suitcases. Anyway, I was able to get the most important things shipped to Jamaica. It was expected to take at least three weeks for the shipment to arrive and then be cleared.

While I had been trying to find an apartment in Jamaica for a few months, I still did not find one before I left Barbados. So, there I was, with a large shipment of belongings on the way and nowhere to put them.

Anyway, I had the peace of God and so I was not worried about any of this. I knew that I had to leave Barbados right away, in order to get to the schools of interest in time to register my sons for the next academic year.

Another perfect alignment was the fact that both of my sons had graduated from each of their schools that month and so it was not an interruption of their academic programme in any way. They both had to enter new schools in September. This also helped to confirm that it was an opportune time to go to Jamaica.

When we arrived in Jamaica in the middle of June, we spent some days with friends in St. Andrew, and did some running around to put important things in place. When most things were put into motion, we went to St. Ann to spend some time with my relatives. While we were visiting these relatives, out of the blue, a dear friend and mentor, fondly called Auntie Grace, from St. Andrew called me on the 28th of June and said, "Sophie, I found the perfect place for you." "How soon can you come to see it?" Well, since we had gone to look for apartments together, I knew that she knew what I was looking for. So, I was excited about the prospect. Also, since it was late in the month, I had to make a decision, so that I could take up residence the next month. So, the next morning, I went to St. Andrew, which was a two-and-a-half-hour drive from where I was. The landlady, Mrs. Bell, had driven in from Mandeville, in the middle of the island to meet me. I was very elated to discover that it was a lady that I had known well. I knew her from when I was a university student in the early 1990s. At that time, she and I attended the same Church, which was walking distance from her apartment. She was always a pleasant and positive person, so I felt good about the prospects of renting the apartment from her.

When we went into the apartment, it was furnished and had everything that we needed to move in right away. So, I paid her and told my family the good news. God had used two friends to find a home for us.

We moved in within a few days and it was a good thing that we got the apartment in July instead of August for several reasons. First, I had a lot more running around to do in that parish than I had realized. The second thing was that the shipment had come early! I had felt that I had at least three weeks for my things to arrive from Barbados and be cleared, so I felt that even if I did not find a place before August that would have been fine. However, imagine my surprise in the second week of July, when the lady from the shipping company called me to say that my shipment had arrived and needed to be cleared. I just don't know where I would have put those things if Auntie Grace had not helped me to find the apartment that day.

Here is another story about that apartment. Before I left Barbados, God had told me exactly where to live in Jamaica and where I should fellowship during the re-settling phase there. It was right in the community where I had last resided before I had migrated from Jamaica. I had made strong

My Testimonies

friendships with people from that neighbourhood and the Church which was in the area. It was to be a superb positioning, since my boys grew to love the place and the people from the Church and neighbourhood. This apartment was right in the heart of that community. That Divine revelation was confirmed. In addition, the apartment was in a very central and easily accessible area in the parish. God is faithful!

That is not the end of this blessing. When my shipment arrived, I did not need all of the furnishings that the landlady had in the apartment, since I had some of my own. Thankfully, Mrs. Bell was able to find somewhere to put some of her things that I did not need. God had also told me what to ship and what not to take along. However, we did not miss anything that we did not take, because God had placed us in a well-outfitted apartment. God is concerned about every area of our lives. Sometimes, confusion or anxiety prevents us from knowing what God is leading us to do. In cases like these, we need to reject every negative, doubtful or disobedient spirit and allow God to work it out for us. He can do more than we can ask or imagine, and He sees the full picture, we only see just around us.

We need to let Him lead us instead of leaning to our own understanding. He is a loving Father, who only wants what is good for us. Sometimes, when we do not step out in faith, we miss opportunities and live outside of God's will for our lives. Ask God for confirmation and/or discuss it with a spiritual leader before you step out and trust God to always do what is good for you and then let Him work it out for your purpose to be fulfilled on the earth.

Your Testimony

Chapter 8:
Financial Provision

My cooking gas had run out for some time, and I had been cautiously using my hotplate, because I did not want a high electricity bill. By May 2014, my friend Grace, who I knew from childhood and who had been positioned by God to help me re-adjust to life in Jamaica was going overseas for a few weeks on a work- related trip.

The day before she left, she drove up to my home and after wishing me a good couple of weeks while she was away, she put an envelope in my hands and said she wanted me to have that in case anything came up while she was away. It was J$9,500. It was not J$10,000 0r J$8,000, but exactly the amount of money that I needed to purchase a 100lb cylinder of cooking gas. Remember, I had neither asked her for any money nor told her how much the cooking gas would cost. God had seen our need and moved on her heart to give me this money to get this important need met. He once again displayed His supernatural providence.

One day in February 2015 I went to visit Auntie Grace (another Grace) who has been a mentor to me for many years. I had not gone to see her for a few weeks. So, one mid-morning, I went to visit her, primarily to use her computer, since mine was down at the time. I had also planned to fellowship with her and to pray for her regarding some of her health challenges while I was there with her.

We talked for a while and then I set off to get some work done on the computer. After about two hours or so, I felt that it was almost time to go. I had been fasting that morning and so I said to her that I wanted to pray with her before I had something to eat. I was also praying and believing God for a breakthrough in my finances that day as I fasted and prayed. I recalled saying to the Lord earlier that morning that I would need about J$5,000 more to do something important and to pay a bill that day.

After I had used the computer, I sat with my friend and began to pray for her to be healed, for her family and for God's peace and strength to envelope her. I prayed as I was led by the Holy Spirit, and she was really moved in her spirit as I prayed.

After we had prayed, she asked how I was getting through with my bills and so on, since at the time, I was not working, except for the ministry related work and a few book sales here and there. So, I shared with her a bit and basically said that God had been seeing us through. I did not say that I needed the J$5,000, nor did I ask her for anything. However, as I prepared to leave, she went into her room and got something to give to me. She said something about being blessed with some money and thought she would like me to have some of it and use it to get something for myself and my sons. When I opened the envelope as I walked out of the house, I saw a J$5,000 bill in the envelope. It was miraculous because she did not even know that I was short that day or how much I had told the Lord that I needed to cover my projected expenses. In addition, a J$5,000 was a rare item at that time. We mainly used J$1,000 bills for large sums of money in Jamaica. God had come through for me again with exactly what I needed, as I had followed His leading and prayed with my friend in her time of sickness and physical weakness.

Your Testimony

Chapter 9:
In His Care

On April 8, 2015, I was in the care of my Heavenly Father. First, one of my good friends was available to watch my sons, Mateo and Mykel, and so I was able to go and sort out some very important business. I was led to fast from the evening before as I organized my thoughts and plans for the day to come. I began the day with the usual morning chores and the tried my best to leave home by mid-morning, so that I could get through with what I needed to do that day.

First, I had to go to the head office of the organization where I worked, in order sort out an important matter. After dealing with the issue, I went to the main road and waited for a taxi to get to Crossroads in Kingston, Jamaica. On my way to Crossroads, only the driver and I were in the taxi. So, he began to tell me about some work that he needed to do on his vehicle. He later told me that he was going directly to sort out the vehicle as soon as he let me off at Crossroads. On hearing this, I thought it would be good if he was heading in the direction of my next destination, so I asked him if he would be travelling along Half-Way-Tree Road to

My Testimonies

get to the mechanic that he was going to use. As it happened, he was heading my way. Therefore, I offered him the fare for that leg of the journey if I could continue with him. This was especially good because it had begun to rain and I did not like getting soaked in the rain. I then told him that I was actually going to Beechwood Avenue to deliver something to the Observer Newspaper.

As we travelled along to our destination, he found another passenger who was going in our direction. Incidentally, that passenger was also going to Beechwood Avenue. Therefore, I asked the driver to take us down to that road, which he did. This was great because I didn't have to walk in the rain from the main road to the Observer Newspaper building.

After conducting my business there, the rain had stopped, and I decided to walk up Beechwood Avenue to Half-Way-Tree Road. On reaching that main road, I felt led in my spirit to look around to see exactly what was near to my location. As it happened, I was just three buildings away from a friend who had promised to buy one of my books. This is someone who is very hard to reach by telephone and who is often in meetings or away overseas. However, he was there when I called and was able to pay for the book as promised. Furthermore, he was heading in my general direction and so, I got a ride back to Crossroads so that I could go to my next destination, which was Liguanea. I was heading to Jamaica House of Prayer for a lunch hour meditation and prayer meeting. I was able to get transportation readily and directly to Liguanea. However, by then one of the straps on my sandals came loose, but I did not panic, because I knew that the road that led up to the Jamaica House of Prayer had a shoe repair shop. So, I decided to go straight to the prayer session and then get my shoe repaired afterwards. If I didn't get the ride in the taxi to Beechwood Avenue or the ride to Crossroads with my friend, my sandals would have burst out in the rain while I was walking along the road with no shoemaker nearby. Praise God for His providential care.

When I got to Jamaica House of Prayer, the prayer session was intense with earnest and strategic prayers being made about critical current issues in the nation. As we prayed, I knew that we were being led by God to pray according to His will. That day was further enhanced when an instrumental spiritual and social activist entered the prayer room for us to pray in agreement about some important issues that were being addressed by her group of activists. This was amazing because early in the morning I felt led to watch one of Jamaica's morning television programmes and she was on the show addressing some of the same issues that we were to pray about.

God is awesome and His ways are past finding out. However, as we trust and follow Him each day, He will truly direct our path and order our steps.

Chapter 10:
Miraculous Car Repair

It was the year 2018. I was living in Jamaica, and I was working at Empowered Living Services and Supplies. I had bought a lovely white Toyota Belta. I really loved that car, but I rarely drove it to remote parts of the country because it had a small engine and was not very good on driving up hills.

However, one weekend a WhatsApp prayer group that I was a part of, was having a retreat and I was invited to go with them to St. Ann. This meant that I would have had to drive for two hours from Kingston to Runaway Bay in St. Ann. As I drove to and from the retreat, I could hear the pressure on the engine. Anyway, we got to the retreat and back without any problems.

However, several days after the retreat, the radiator started acting up. When I drove it to the mechanic, he showed me a broken valve near the engine. The part was made of hard plastic, and he believed the pressure had built up in the valve and broken it.

First, he tried to weld the part, but it was unsuccessful. I tried to buy the part, but none of the auto parts stores or car repair places had the part. One place said they could order it but that would take at least three weeks for it to get to Jamaica. This was very disconcerting.

During my quest to find the auto part a gentleman told me about a metal works place that could build the part for me. The place was near to Crossroads in Kingston. When I got to Crossroads, I felt led to stop and get something to eat. So, I had a patty and cocoa bread, which was mouth-watering.

After that I went to the metal works place and one of the workmen came and took the old part out of the car to go and build the necessary car part for me.

While we were there discussing how he was going to build the part a man drove into the car park with the exact same part that I needed in his hand. I was lost for words. As it happened, the man was a mechanic who wanted that same part built for a car that he was working on. So, he was able to explain how to build the part. It was definitely a wonder.

The first miracle was that he had the identical part that I needed for my car. The second miracle was that he assisted in the design of the car part. The third miracle was that he was the mechanic that I needed to repair my car. He knew just how to fix my car. A noteworthy point was that if I had not stopped to eat, I would not have been there the exact time that he walked in.

My Testimonies

God enabled the repair of my car in one day instead of waiting three weeks to import the part. The other blessing was that the metal part was far stronger that the original hard plastic part. One other very important blessing was that the part did not break while I was driving on the long, lonely highway to get to and from Runaway Bay. Praise God for His hand in this situation.

Chapter 11:
Amazing Deal

I have been a member of New Dimensions Ministries (NDM), in St. Michael Barbados since 2005. NDM is a dynamic, uplifting and Holy Spirit filled Church. One Sunday in June 2011, Zoanne Evans (PhD), who lectures at the University of the West Indies and who is also an author, artist and fellow believer, announced in Church that she was having a writer's workshop. She wanted to help high school and tertiary level students to improve their writing skills. When I heard the announcement, I knew right away that I wanted to take the course. My friend Shelley Ward and I both decided to sign up. Shelley was always writing poems and even short stories. On the other hand, I had received a prophetic word that I would use the gift in my hands to glorify God. As I thought about it, the only thing I could think of as a gift in my hands was my writing. So, we joined the writers' workshop.

Zoanne was very good at honing our skill in writing. We had meaningful discussions as we learned how to improve our writing. It was a good time of interactive learning.

My Testimonies

The highlight of the workshop was when she brought in another published author (Zoanne being a published writer), to talk to us about getting our books published. The guest speaker mentioned that she used Xlibris publishing company to publish her book. Zoanne talked about using A and A Printing in Florida to publish her book. It was very exciting as we learned about and explored different publishing options.

The interesting thing was that when Zoanne told us how much money she paid to print 500 copies of her book, it was the same amount as what I had stashed away for a rainy day. However, I decided to raise some of the money to publish the book instead of using only my savings. So, NDM allowed me to sell cake to raise some of the money. It was well supported as I sold cake for several weeks.

Regarding the book that I was publishing, I had a few poems that I had written, and I was always writing out my prayers, so I decided to write a book of poems and prayers, which was my first book, "Divinely Empowered; Poems and Prayers for your Inspiration."

So, I wrote the book and got some friends; Greta and Paula, to edit it for me. Also, Zoanne Evans drew three lovely pictures for the book to really give it a beautiful finish, like the icing on the cake. I sent the manuscript to A and A Printing and got my first self-published book in November 2011. The books sold well.

I was busy selling my book at Church and directly to people I knew, and it was selling reasonably well. Then one day I decided to check out Xlibris, the self-publishing company, which the guest presenter at the writer's workshop had mentioned that she uses. So, I had sent them an email, expressing my interest in being published with one of their attractive self-publishing packages, some of which were reasonably priced.

One night in December 2011, I was in the kitchen preparing dinner when my phone rang. The caller was from Xlibris, and he was telling me that they had a 50% discount packages for those who signed up with them before the end of the month. I was engrossed in my conversation but kept cooking. It was just the opportunity I had hoped for. As this conversation progressed there was a sudden downpour of rain. This was a very typical way that it rains in Barbados, a sudden downpour of rain, which stops in a few minutes. If you had clothes on the line outside, this would be very disconcerting, as you rush out to pick them up, while getting soaked in the rain, which suddenly stops, leaving you and your laundry soaked. I call it "God throwing down a bucket of water."

So, there I was, cooking and talking and "God threw down a bucket of water." The back door of the house needed to be closed when the rain falls to avoid getting the entrance soaked and help prevent the children from sliding in the water and falling.

So, since the back door was open, I rushed out to the garage to get the mop to go and wipe up the back entrance. As I was rushing out the door, I glimpsed that the gas hose between the stove and the gas bottle was on fire. I quickly went and turned off the stove. The stove had two bad burners and I believe that was the reason for the fire.

Brother, sister, friend, if God didn't throw down that bucket of water I would not be here today. As I wiped up the water, I thanked God for delivering us from an explosion.

Needless to say, I accepted the offer from Xlibris and got my 50% off book publishing contract. I truly believe that the devil did not want me to publish the book, but grace and mercy came to my rescue.

Chapter 12:
Miraculous Car Sale

Since November of 2022 I did a service and mechanical check on my car "Sparkle" and by December, I decided that it was time to sell it and get a younger car to replace it. This was also because the paint on the roof and front of the car was stripping badly. One mechanic said it could cost up to US $2,500.00 to paint it. This was definitely not an option for me.

The first thing that I did was to get the vehicle valued. According to the valuation, the car was worth US $5,750.00. Which sounded good. So, I placed an advertisement in the newspaper US $5000.00. After several days of responding to potential buyers, none of them wanted to pay more than US $3,500.00 for the car.

Therefore, I placed a for sale sign on it and a few persons asked about it, but none wanted to buy the car at the price range that I was hoping for. Eventually when old for sale sign faded out, I replaced it with a new for sale sign but this time I did not put how much money I was asking for it on the for-sale sign.

By April, one man told me over the phone that he would pay me he would pay US $3,000.00 for the car, but when he saw the striping of the paint, he wanted to decrease his offer to US $2,500.00. That was definitely a no for me. So, I drove away, wondering and pondering if the car was ever going to get sold, but I kept the for-sale sign on the car.

Anyway, on Thursday, May 11,2023, I was on my way home from work, and I decided to stop at the Esso Service Station in Black Rock, St. Michael. Somehow, I had forgotten to buy bread the day before and so I turned in and parked. The news had just started so I decided to sit in the car and listen to the news before entering the convenience store.

As I sat there a young man came to my window and asked me how much I was asking for the car, and I told him US $3,500.00 we negotiated a bit and then he looked at the engine and told me that he was going to get his friend, who was a mechanic.

I told him to meet me at UWI, Cave Hill, where I was going walking with my friend Glenda. Within about 20 minutes the two of them showed up at UWI. They examined the car, and we took it for a test drive. After which, we negotiated on the final price and then they left to get the money. After another 20 minutes they came back with the money and we both filled out the vehicle sale documents. The car was sold.

The next day, I borrowed some money to help pay off the difference that I owed to the car dealership where I had bought Sparkle. Two weeks before the sale, I had gone into the used car lot to see how much I owed and how much I could get to borrow to buy a replacement vehicle. So, they were aware of the price range of the vehicle that I was looking for.

After we paid off the loan balance, I was ready to go home when Mateo said, "Mom let's go by the used car lot and see what types of vehicles they have for sale."

I had checked with the salesperson the day before to see if they had anything in my price range. However, he said they didn't. Nevertheless, I decided to follow Mateo's suggestion and go to see what vehicles they had.

As soon as I opened the door, my salesperson blurted out, "I was just going to give you a call. We just got two vehicles in your price range." It was a miracle.

He took us outside to look at the first one. It was in excellent condition! It was a 2016 Kia Picanto, I named her "Grace" for several reasons. Two women named Grace had been rich blessings to my life. In addition, we were studying about Grace at Church, and I was able to purchase the car through God's grace.

We spent the rest of the afternoon filling out some car sale paperwork, being thankful that a miracle had happened. After several months of waiting, I sold a car one day and purchased a replacement one the next day. God's timing is perfect!

God is concerned about every area of our lives. He wants us to prosper and be in health as our souls prosper. May God cause all of our souls to prosper in Jesus' name.

Author Contact Page

You may contact Sophia (BSc, MBA, Cert Trainer [TVET]) regarding any queries, book orders, or *Business and Personal Development Training Seminars/Workshops* by using the information below:

Researcher, Trainer, Motivational Speaker/ Personal Development and Financial Advisor *E-Mail:*
<u>sophiadvisor@gmail.com</u>

<u>Training is Offered On:</u>

- Customer Service, Sales, and Marketing
- Life Skills, Professionalism and Career Development
- Comprehensive Personal Development Training
- Leadership
- Parenting
- Financial Planning
- Business Management and Developing a New or an Existing Business Enterprise

Sophia is also the author of:

- ❖ *Divinely Empowered; Poems and Prayers for your Inspiration*
- ❖ *Living Above the Norm; Meaningful and Victorious Living with Christ*
- ❖ *Parenting Matters*
- ❖ *Happy and Healthy Child; Doses of Motivation for Young People*